Try again,

Story by Annette Smith
Illustrated by Priscilla Cutter

Hannah and her friend Kim
were getting ready
for the gym meet.
Kim jumped up and down
on the trampoline to warm up.

Hannah waved to Mom.

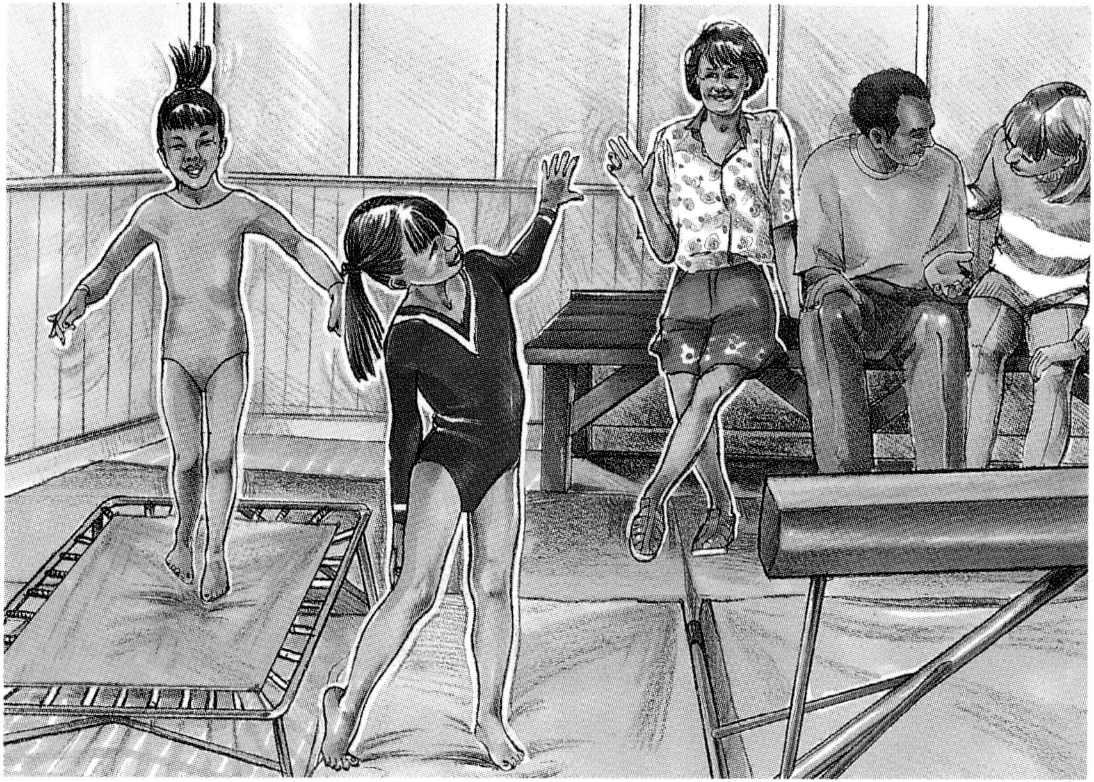

"Are you all ready?"
said the coach. "Line up, please.
We are going to start now."

The boys and girls
ran to line up.
"Do your best," said the coach
to all the children.

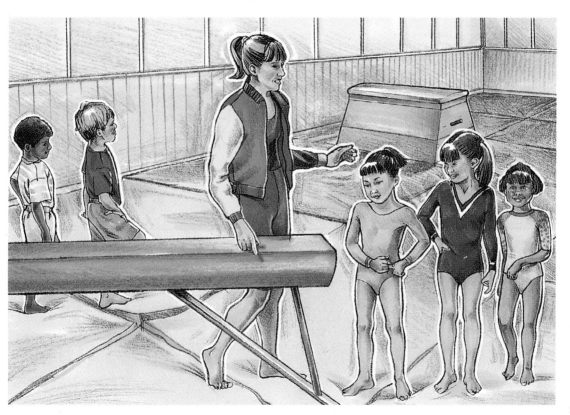

Kim went first.
She walked slowly
along the beam
and jumped off
onto the mat.

"Good girl, Kim"
said the coach.

Hannah was next.
She looked over
at Mom
and smiled.

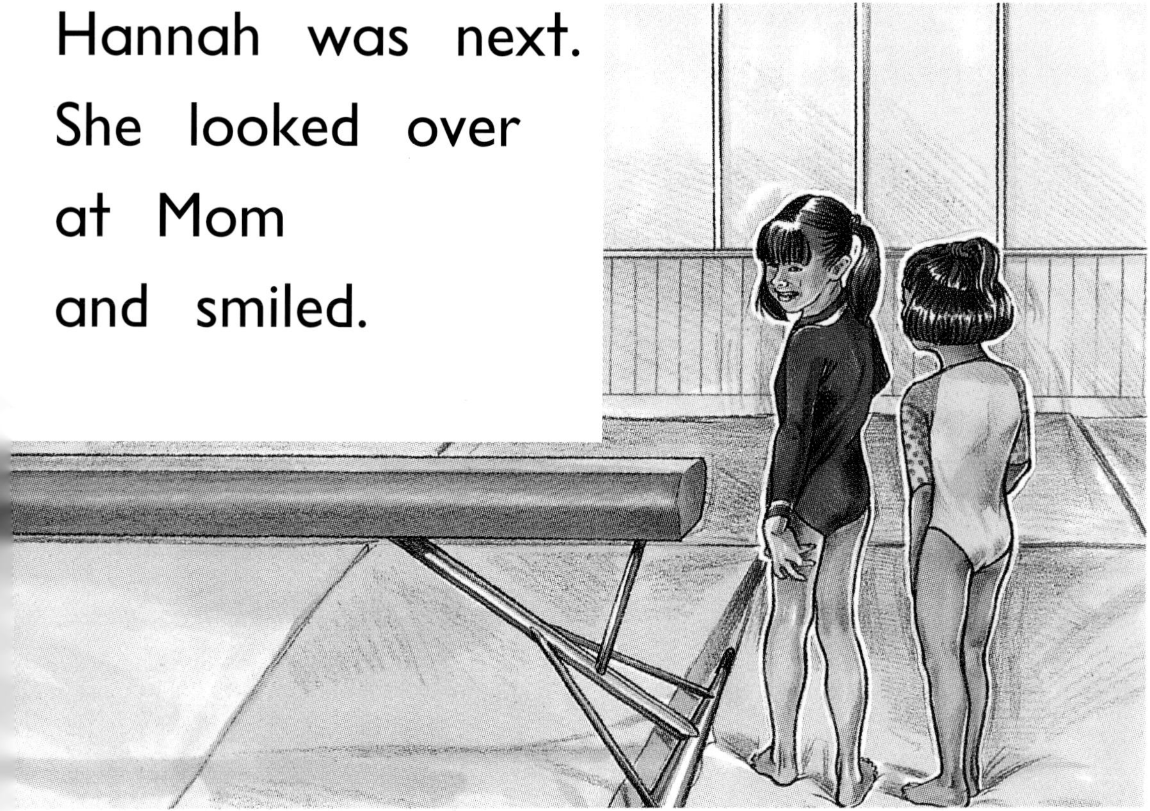

Hannah walked along the beam, too.

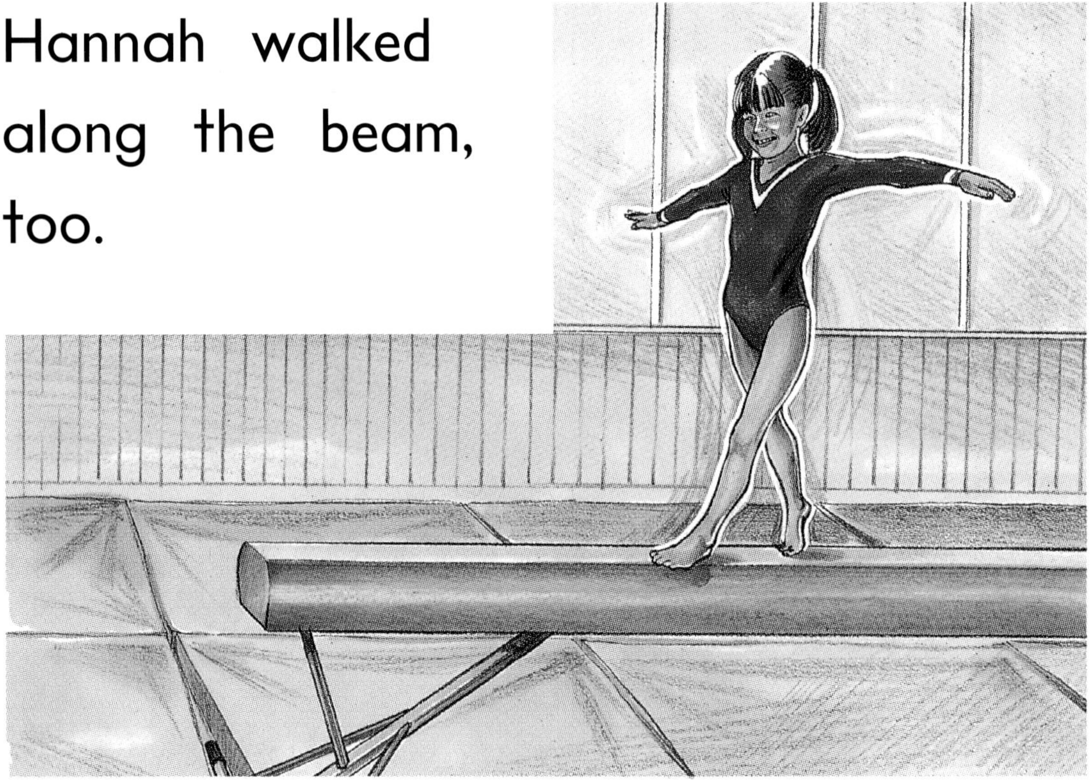

Then she turned around slowly . . .
and walked back.

"Well done, Hannah," said the coach.

Everyone in the line
had a turn on the beam.

Then the girls
had to go on the bars.

This time, it was Hannah's turn
to go first.

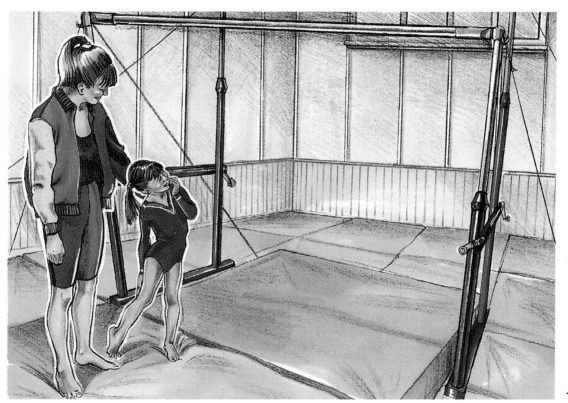

The coach
helped Hannah
up to the bar.
She began
to swing
but then . . .

she fell down
onto the mat!

"Come on, Hannah,"
said the coach.
"You can start again.
I will help you
to get back up."

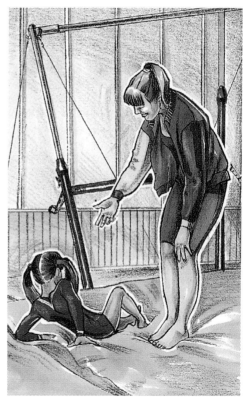

"No," said Hannah.
"I can't do it."

"Yes, you can!"
said Kim.

"Don't give up now,"
said the coach.

Hannah began
to swing again,
and this time
she did **not**
fall off.

The moms and dads
all cheered.
"Well done!"
said the coach.
"I'm glad that
you didn't give up."